T0278731

365

Thoughts
for Connecting
with Nature

whitestar

365
Thoughts
for Connecting
with Nature

CONTENTS

LIST OF CONTRIBUTORS - ILLUSTRATION CREDITS

THE BEGINNING OF A NEW LIFE

The events of these recent years have touched us all. The pandemic, with its terrible toll of human sufferings and economic anxieties; wars; and natural disasters have shown us how important it is to face everything with clarity, without letting ourselves spiral into panic. We cannot always determine or influence what is happening around us, but it is important that we do not abandon ourselves to the mercy of events, that we focus our efforts and resources on maintaining balance and helping ourselves and those who need it most.

Today mindfulness is therefore of the utmost importance to promote both individual and collective well-being. We meditate on the past to learn something, not to waste energy and joy in regrets and remorse. We appreciate the present because it is the Now; it is the moment in which we live and breathe. We make sense of the future because it will become our present, that place in time where we will find ourselves in a minute, a day, a month, or a year. All this should not anguish us, because if we understand how to live every single moment thoroughly, in due course we will be ready to do it.

Meditating means breathing here and now, without rush or anxiety; we can do it with our eyes shut, looking inward, or by turning our gaze to Mother Nature, who always shows us that everything knows how to adapt to its season, accepting the passage of time and evolving or changing as needed. However, meditating in solitude is not always so easy, which is why reflections and considerations of others are useful. We can seek advice from people who are or have been more attentive and sensitive to this all-too-human need to learn what is natural, who have experienced what it means to breathe and keep one's balance. When looking for "masters of meditation" to follow, we are naturally inclined to think of Buddhist masters, saints, or mystical figures that we perceive as "superior beings." That could be good, but we should not stop there. Artists too—be they poets, painters, or writers—show their same heightened sensitivity, not only in their works, but also in the way they explain what they see, hear, or feel when facing the majesty of Nature. Those who have lived in nature and with nature can only champion it, and invite us to return to its simplicity, to respect its simple rules, which benefit us and the whole of which we are a part.

Sometimes precious teachings on how to live in the here and now are imparted by those who distinguished themselves in the defense of human rights or in the study of science. Should this come as a surprise? Let's stop for a while and ponder it. Those who have fought against injustices or have studied the mysteries of the universe have understood one basic principle no one can ignore: nature is the source of life, and life blossoms and prospers in many forms that shape this very world in which they move and find their reason to exist in perfect unity. The short and precious teachings collected in the following pages, therefore, have this precise purpose: day by day, they make manifest the *premises and consequences of that "conscious attention" to the world that sometimes is so difficult for us to achieve, but that can help us feel that we belong to it at every stage and in every moment of our life. This is mindfulness: being aware of ourselves and of the reality that surrounds us here and now, we face reality and ourselves with a non-judgmental attitude, knowing that this is the way to feel better as individuals and as a community.*

The evocative images that follow the succession of months will help us "see" how to direct our consciousness: we will feel that every season has its beauty and usefulness in the annual cycle; that every animal takes care of itself and knows how to do whatever is necessary to survive; that mountains—home to a myriad of living beings—do not necessarily have to be climbed, but simply admired for their majesty, and thanked for the peace they give to our soul; that water can flow at different speeds or be still, and yet lose none of its importance for life. We could go on indefinitely, and each of us would find different but equally valid meanings in all those images. This is a point to be made. Having this positive attitude of mind, we must turn our gaze to the reality that surrounds us and develop our ability to perceive ourselves in the flow of life, looking inside and outside of ourselves and considering negative thoughts only for what they are: creations of the mind and not actual realities. Distinguishing what is real from what we fear is key to the reduction of anxiety and stress (evils that increasingly affect people of all sexes and of all ages), and to achieve resilience, well-being, and happiness.

Jon Kabat-Zinn—to whom we owe the Mindfulness Based Stress Reduction (MBSR) program—once claimed "Mindfulness is paying attention, intentionally, in the present and without judgment," and "Awareness is simply the art of living present to oneself." And he is right. Mindfulness is nothing unattainable: it is something we have to learn to do, something we can learn, even if it doesn't come as natural to us as it is for newborn children. What are we trying to say here? Concentration on breathing helps us take the first step: when we are born, instinct spontaneously leads us to breathe; now effortlessly focusing on our breath is the first step to get back the harmony we've lost with nature, to be in tune with ourselves and with everything to which we belong. Breathing is just the beginning; then we move on to perceive our own body, then we concentrate on sensations, then on thoughts, up to the world that surrounds us. Through meditation we come to experience conscious attention in every moment of our daily life, and acquire the ability to fully enjoy what gives us pleasure, and accept what we do not like, being resilient when necessary. In short, mindfulness becomes the state of mind that allows us to live in the best way possible.

1ST

January

Whatever the present moment contains,
accept it as if you had chosen it. Always work with it, not against it.
Make it your friend and ally, not your enemy.
This will miraculously transform your whole life.

– Eckhart Tolle

JANUARY

2ND

January

Every being holds within itself a treasure
that just begs to be discovered.

– *Matthieu Ricard*

3RD

January

Write it on your heart that every day
is the best day in the year.

– *Ralph Waldo Emerson*

4TH

January

In the confrontation between
the stream and the rock,
the stream always wins, not through
strength but by perseverance.

– Buddha

5TH

January

No man ever steps
in the same river twice.

– Heraclitus

6TH

January

To the quiet mind
all things are possible.

– Meister Eckhart

7TH

January

Adaptability is not imitation.
It means power of resistance
and assimilation.

– Mahatma Gandhi

8ᵀᴴ

January

Travel makes one modest.
You see what a tiny place
you occupy in the world.

– *Gustave Flaubert*

9ᵀᴴ

January

Paths are made by walking.

– *Franz Kafka*

10TH

January

Trees are the earth's endless effort
to speak to the listening heaven.

– Rabindranath Tagore

11TH

January

Wherever you are, be there totally.

– Eckhart Tolle

12TH

January

He who returns from a journey
is not the same as he who left.

– Chinese proverb

13TH

January

Do not seek to follow in the footsteps
of the wise; seek what they sought.

– Matsuo Bashō

14TH

January

The most difficult thing in life
is to know yourself.

– Thales of Miletus

15TH

January

Do not brood over your past mistakes
and failures, as this will
only fill your mind with grief,
regret, and depression.
Do not repeat them in the future.

– Sivananda

16TH
January

Meditation brings wisdom;
lack of meditation leaves ignorance.
Know well what leads you forward
and what holds you back, and choose
the path that leads to wisdom.

— *Buddha*

17TH
January

In what room should you meditate?
In your own heart.

— *Eihei Dōgen*

18TH

January

If we had no winter,
the spring would not be so pleasant;
if we did not sometimes taste of adversity,
prosperity would not be so welcome.

– Anne Bradstreet

19TH

January

The sky is the ultimate art gallery just above us.

– Ralph Waldo Emerson

20TH

January

I have to get rid of time and live in the present,
since there is no other time than this wonderful moment.

– Alda Merini

21ST

January

Beauty is not in the face; beauty is a light in the heart.

– Kahlil Gibran

22ND

January

There is no greater freedom than freedom to be all of oneself.

– Alan W. Watts

23RD

January

You can always live happily, as it is up to you to follow
the right path and think and act accordingly.

– Marcus Aurelius

24TH

January

See simplicity in the complicated.
Achieve greatness in little things.

– Lao Tzu

25TH

January

The appearance of things
changes according to the emotions;
and thus we see magic and beauty
in them, while the magic and beauty
are really in ourselves.

– Kahlil Gibran

26TH

January

Only in quietness do we possess
our own minds and discover
the resources of the inner life.

– Helen Keller

27TH

January

It is not enough to have pure hands;
one must have a pure mind.

– Thales of Miletus

28TH

January

There are those who give with joy,
and that joy is their reward.

– Kahlil Gibran

29TH
January

Life is a cycle, always in motion,
if good times have moved on,
so will times of trouble.

— *Indian proverb*

30TH
January

There is no such thing as bad weather,
only different kinds of good weather.

— *John Ruskin*

31ST
January

Like the seeds, my soul also needs
the hidden tillage of this season.

– *Giuseppe Ungaretti*

1ST

February

The purpose of meditation practice is not enlightenment;
it is to pay attention even at extraordinary times, to be of the present,
nothing-but-in-the-present, to bear this mindfulness
of now into each event of ordinary life.

– *Peter Matthiessen*

FEBRUARY

2ND

February

Does this path have a heart? If it does,
the path is good; if it doesn't, it is of no use.

– Carlos Castaneda

3RD

February

Time will never be truly ours
if we don't start being masters
of ourselves.

– Lucius Annaeus Seneca

4TH

February

Smiling means living like a wave,
like a leaf, accepting your fate.
It means dying in one form
and being reborn in another.
It means accepting –
accepting oneself, accepting fate.

– Cesare Pavese

5TH

February

May the rays of dawn
take your night dreams
– the most beautiful ones –
by the hand, and lead
them to reality.

– Tibetan proverb

6TH

February

Meditation is not a means to an end.
It is both the means and the end.

– Jiddu Krishnamurti

7TH

February

Yesterday I was clever, so I wanted to change the world.
Today I am wise, so I am changing myself.

– Jalal al-Din Rumi

8TH

February

Life is a journey,
not a destination.

– *Ralph Waldo Emerson*

9TH

February

There seems to be in man,
as in birds, a need for migration,
a vital need to feel elsewhere.

– *Marguerite Yourcenar*

10TH

February

Part of being optimistic is keeping one's head pointed toward the sun, one's feet moving forward.

– *Nelson Mandela*

11TH

February

Even though you tripped and fell,
that doesn't mean you've taken the wrong path.

– Zen proverb

12TH

February

There is no greater joy for me
than looking at the sky on a clear night
with an attention so concentrated
that all my other thoughts disappear.

– Simone Weil

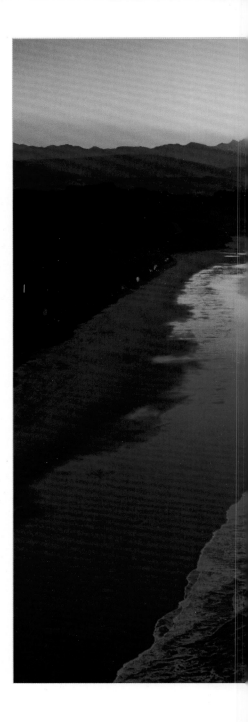

13TH

February

A Warrior of the Light
has no certainties, he just has a path
to follow, a path to which he tries
to adapt depending on the season.

– Paulo Coelho

14TH

February

Differences are not intended to separate,
to alienate. We are different precisely
in order to realize our need
of one another.

– Desmond Tutu

15TH
February

Close your eyes, and you will see.

– Joseph Joubert

16TH
February

Paying attention to your breath
takes your attention away
from thoughts and creates space.
It is a way of generating awareness.

– Eckhart Tolle

17TH

February

The day was filled with lightning; but now the stars will come out,
the silent stars.

– Giovanni Pascoli

18TH

February

If you truly love nature, you will find beauty everywhere.

– Vincent van Gogh

19TH

February

Happiness is like the mountain summit.
It is sometimes hidden by clouds,
but we know it is there.

– Helen Keller

20TH

February

It is the climb itself
which is the adventure,
not just standing at the top.

– Jon Kabat-Zinn

21ST

February

Do not dwell in the past,
do not dream of the future, concentrate
the mind on the present moment.

– Buddha

22ND

February

Man is like a tree; and after
every winter, there comes the spring
with new leaves and new vigor.

– Vasco Pratolini

23RD

February

You have no choice but to be
who you are and where you are.

– *Ikkyū Sōjun*

24TH

February

Accepting the fact that you are
responsible for whatever you are
is the beginning of awareness.

– *Osho*

25TH

February

The most beautiful emotions
are the ones that you cannot explain.

– *Charles Baudelaire*

26TH

February

People don't notice whether it's winter
or summer when they're happy.

– *Anton Chekhov*

27TH

February

In rivers, the water that you touch
is the last of what has passed
and the first of that which comes;
so with present time.

– Leonardo da Vinci

28/29TH

February

The waters of a river adapt themselves
to whatever route proves possible,
but never forget their one objective:
the sea.

– Paulo Coelho

1ST

March

When you do your best, you learn to accept yourself.
But you have to be aware and learn from your mistakes.
Learning from your mistakes means you practice,
look honestly at the results, and keep practicing.
This increases your awareness.

– Don Miguel Ruiz

MARCH

2ND

March

To see a World in a Grain of Sand.
And a Heaven in a Wild Flower.
Hold Infinity in the palm of your hand.

– William Blake

3RD

March

I have learned to seek my happiness by
limiting my desires, rather than
in attempting to satisfy them.

– John Stuart Mill

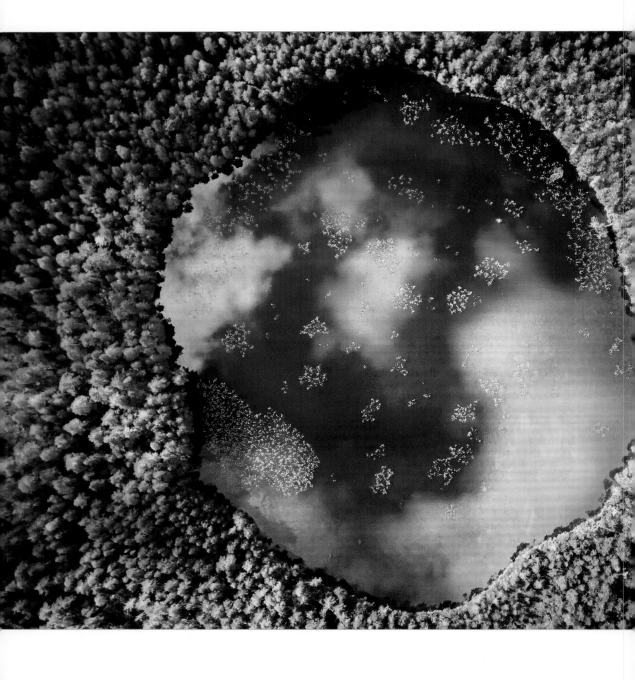

4TH

March

It's not what you look at that matters,
it's what you see.

– Henry David Thoreau

5TH

March

Nature is the art of God.

– Ralph Waldo Emerson

6TH
March

Stop thinking,
and end your problems.

– Lao Tzu

7TH
March

The future torments us,
the past holds us back;
that is why the present eludes ourselves.

– Gustave Flaubert

8TH
March

Zen in its essence is the art of seeing
into the nature of one's own being.

– Daisetsu Teitarō Suzuki

9TH

March

We must use time wisely
and forever realize that the time
is always ripe to do right.

– Nelson Mandela

10TH

March

Kind words can be short
and easy to speak, but their echoes
are truly endless.

– Mother Teresa

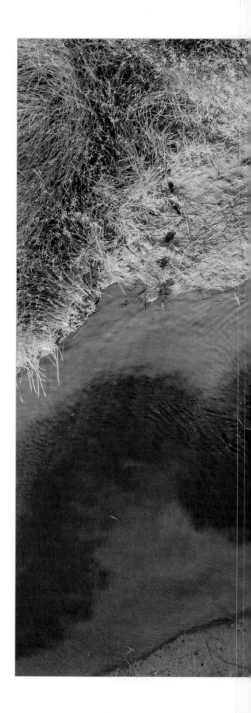

11TH

March

Beauty pleases the eyes only;
sweetness of disposition charms
the soul.

– *Voltaire*

12TH

March

Only the fool walks the path
of life without pausing to observe
the beauties of creation.

– *Tibetan proverb*

13TH

March

The happy life is the one in accordance
with its own nature.

– Lucius Annaeus Seneca

14TH

March

What is success?
It is being able to go to bed
each night with your soul at peace.

– Paulo Coelho

15TH

March

In the midst of difficulty lies opportunity.

– Albert Einstein

16TH

March

Sometimes happiness is hidden in the unknown.

– Victor Hugo

17TH

March

The world is my country,
all mankind are my brethren,
and to do good is my religion.

– Thomas Paine

18TH

March

Travel to discover the countries;
you will find the continent in yourself.

– Thai proverb

19TH
March

Life is not a problem to be solved,
but a reality to be experienced.

– Søren Kierkegaard

20TH
March

Don't give up. You might risk
doing it an hour before the miracle.

– Arab proverb

21ST
March

I am not my thoughts, emotions,
sense perceptions, and experiences.
I am not the content of my life.
I am Life. I am the space in which
all things happen. I am consciousness.
I am the Now. I Am.

– Eckhart Tolle

22ND
March

You are never too young
nor too old to pursue happiness.

– Epicurus

23RD

March

For every minute you are angry
you lose sixty seconds of happiness.

– Ralph Waldo Emerson

24TH

March

Find out who you are and don't be afraid of it.

– Mahatma Gandhi

25TH
March

Who looks outside, dreams; who looks inside, awakes.

– Carl Gustav Jung

26TH
March

Keep your hand open, and you can get everything.
Close it, and you cannot receive anything.

– Taïsen Deshimaru

27TH
March

My soul can find no staircase
to Heaven unless it be through
Earth's loveliness.

– Michelangelo Buonarroti

28TH
March

If what I say resonates with you,
it's merely because we're branches
of the same tree.

– William Butler Yeats

29TH

March

Our body is a boat that will take us
to the other side of the ocean of life.
We must take care of it.

– Vivekananda

30TH

March

We get from the sea what it offers us,
not what we want.

– Erri De Luca

31ST

March

When you cross the entrance arch
to the temple of dreams, there,
right there, is the sea.

– Luis Sepúlveda

1ST

April

Each of us can do something to protect the planet and take care of it.
We must live in such a way that a future is possible for our children
and grandchildren. Our life must be our message.

– Thích Nhất Hạnh

APRIL

2ND

April

If you want to see the top
of the mountain, rise above the cloud.
But if you try to understand the cloud,
close your eyes and think.

– Kahlil Gibran

3RD

April

Everything you can imagine
is real.

– Pablo Picasso

4TH

April

Patience is the companion of wisdom.

– Augustine of Hippo

5TH

April

It is the small joys first of all that are granted us for recreation, for daily relief and disburdenment, not the great ones.

– Hermann Hesse

6TH

April

Great results can be achieved with small forces.

– Sun Tzu

7TH

April

Time is a river which sweeps me along, but I am the river.

– Jorge Luis Borges

8TH
April

One good day plus another good day
equals a good life.

– Isabel Allende

9TH
April

Love, out of love, has descended
into this world in the form of beauty.

– Simone Weil

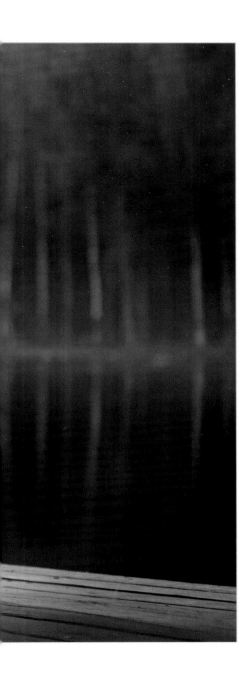

10TH

April

Of all the treasures that wisdom
can amass for happiness, friendship
is the greatest, the most inexhaustible,
the sweetest.

– *Epicurus*

11TH

April

Be like a bee who is happy
with who and what it is,
and do not waste your time
admiring the soaring of eagles.

– *Kahlil Gibran*

12TH

April

The flower doesn't dream of the bee.
It blossoms and the bee comes.

– *Mark Nepo*

13TH

April

The meaning of things lies not in the things themselves,
but in our attitude toward them.

– Antoine de Saint-Exupéry

14TH

April

Love life more than its logic;
only then will you understand its meaning.

– Fyodor Dostoevsky

15ᵀᴴ

April

Everything has beauty, but not everyone sees it.

– Confucius

16ᵀᴴ

April

When a person can't find a deep sense of meaning,
they distract themselves with pleasure.

– Viktor Emil Frankl

17TH

April

Don't judge each day by the harvest
you reap but by the seeds
that you plant.

– Robert Louis Stevenson

18TH

April

We know what we are, but know not what we may be.

– *William Shakespeare*

19TH

April

And joy is everywhere.

– Rabindranath Tagore

20TH

April

Life is a gift, life is happiness. . . .
Every minute could have been an eternity
of happiness!

– *Fyodor Dostoevsky*

21ST

April

Life is a succeof lessons
which must be lived to be understood.

– *Ralph Waldo Emerson*

22ND

April

God is within you. Find it out!

– *Sathya Sai Baba*

23RD

April

To meditate does not mean withdrawing from the world. It means seeing things clearly and deliberately taking different positions with respect to them.

– *Jon Kabat-Zinn*

24TH
April

Sit at the edge of dawn,
the sun will rise for you.
Sit on the edge of the night,
the moon will raise for you.
Sit at the edge of a stream,
a bird will sing to you.
Sit on the edge of silence,
and God will speak to you.

– Vivekananda

25TH

April

Peace comes from within. Do not seek it without.

– Anonymous

26TH

April

Meditation provides a way of learning how to let go.
As we sit, the self we've been trying to construct and make into a nice,
neat package continues to unravel.

– John Welwood

27TH

April

Let us take the muddy path
to get to the clouds.

– *Matsuo Bashō*

28TH

April

Absolute purity consists in not suffering
or using force.

– *Simone Weil*

29TH

April

Sometimes it's necessary to go backward in order to go forward.

– *Martin Luther King*

30TH

April

Storms make trees take deeper roots.

– Anonymous

1ST

May

Any activity in life can become a ritual of love:
eating, walking, talking, playing.
When everything is a ritual of love, you no longer think: you just feel.
Just being alive makes you feel immensely happy.

– Don Miguel Ruiz

2ND

May

No man is free who is not master
of himself.

– Epictetus

3RD

May

The future belongs to those who believe
in the beauty of their dreams.

– Eleanor Roosevelt

4TH

May

Opposites are reconciled,
from apparent chaos a most beautiful
harmony is born, and everything
is generated through contention.

– Heraclitus

5TH

May

The past is history. It no longer exists,
but you are keeping it alive in your
mind through your thoughts. Let it go.
It is not serving you.

– Sonia Ricotti

6TH

May

There are many things in life
that will catch your eye, but only
a few will catch your heart.
Pursue these.

– Michael Patrick Nolan

7TH

May

Happiness is when what you think,
what you say,
and what you do are in harmony.

– Mahatma Gandhi

8TH

May

There is no failure except
in no longer trying.

– Elbert Hubbard

9TH

May

It does not matter how slowly
you go, as long as you do not stop.

– Confucius

10TH

May

Even for the simple flight of a butterfly
all the sky is necessary.

– Paul Claudel

11TH

May

Happiness is a butterfly,
which, when pursued,
is always just beyond your grasp,
but which, if you will sit down quietly,
may alight upon you.

– Nathaniel Hawthorne

12TH

May

Don't worry if others
don't appreciate you. Worry if you don't
appreciate yourself.

– *Confucius*

13TH

May

We cannot choose who we are,
but we can wish to improve ourselves.

– *Matthieu Ricard*

14TH

May

The curious paradox is that when I accept myself
just as I am, then I change.

– Carl Rogers

15TH

May

Accepting and adapting is the right psychological
attitude whenever something changes.

– Umberto Veronesi

16TH

May

Two things cannot be in one place.
Where you tend a rose, my lad,
a thistle cannot grow.

– Frances Hodgson Burnett

17TH

May

Nothing is a waste of time
if you use the experience wisely.

– Auguste Rodin

18TH
May

The rhythm of the body,
the melody of the mind,
and the harmony of the soul
create the symphony of life.

– B.K.S. Iyengar

19TH
May

Each is the proper guardian
of his own health, whether bodily,
or mental and spiritual.

– John Stuart Mill

20TH

May

Some things you miss because
they're so tiny you overlook them.
But some things you don't see
because they're so huge.

– Robert Maynard Pirsig

21ST

May

A world of grief and pain:
Flowers bloom;
Even then.

– Kobayashi Issa

22ND

May

Happiness, knowledge,
not in another place, but this place,
not for another hour, but this hour.

– *Walt Whitman*

23RD

May

Count the flowers in your garden,
never the falling leaves.

– Romano Battaglia

24TH

May

Nothing great was ever achieved
without enthusiasm.

– Henry David Thoreau

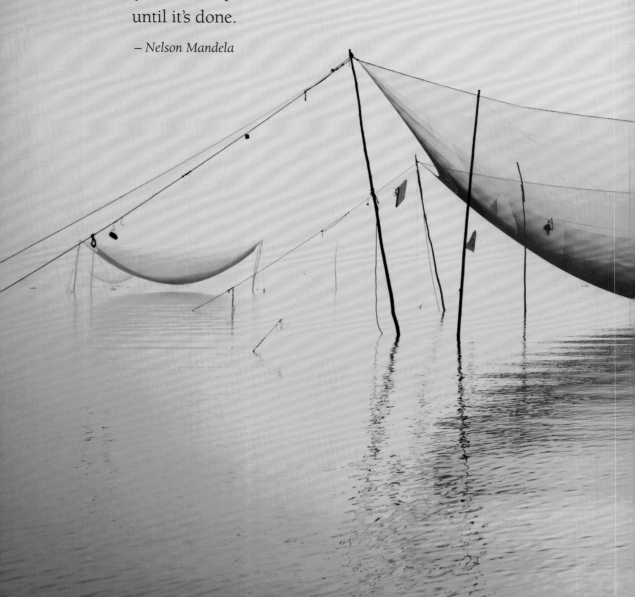

25TH

May

It always seems impossible
until it's done.

– *Nelson Mandela*

26TH
May

Now I am going out among people;
it may be that I do not know anything,
but a new life has begun.

– Fyodor Dostoevsky

27TH
May

Strength does not come from
physical capacity. It comes from
an indomitable will.

– Mahatma Gandhi

28TH

May

If you do not change direction,
you may end up where you are heading.

– Lao Tzu

29TH

May

Life must be lived, not thought about.
Otherwise, it denies itself and shows
itself as an empty shell.

– Eugenio Montale

30TH

May

A man who dares to waste
one hour of time has not discovered
the value of life.

– *Charles Darwin*

31ST

May

To live a full life depends only on me.

– *Lucius Annaeus Seneca*

1ST

June

Youth is happy because it has the capacity to see beauty.
Anyone who keeps the ability to see beauty never grows old.

– Franz Kafka

JUNE

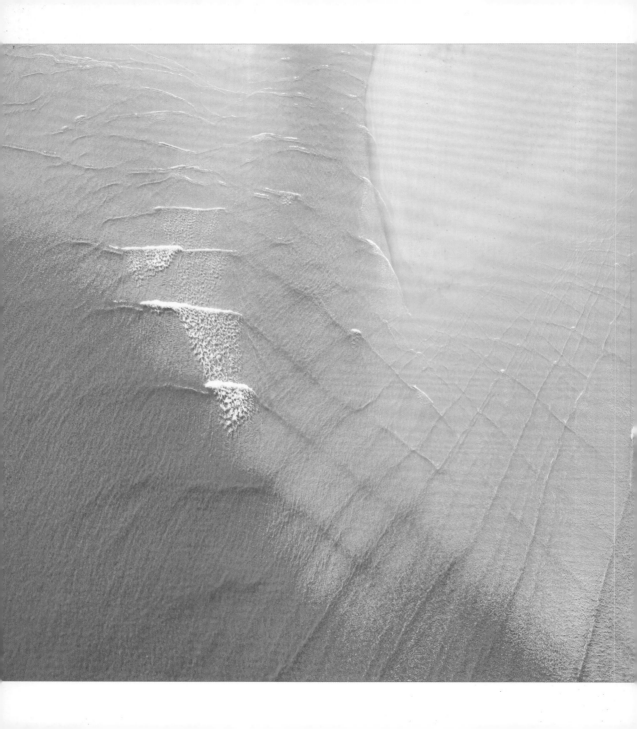

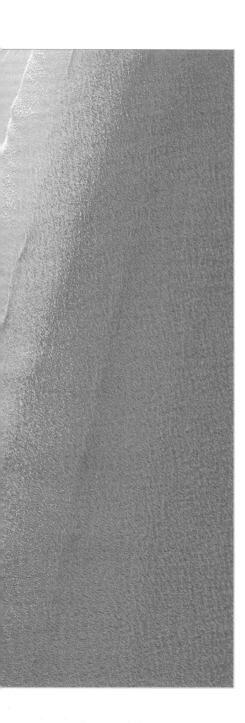

2ND

June

Free man, you will always cherish the sea!
The sea is your mirror; you contemplate
your soul in the infinite unrolling
of its billows.

– Charles Baudelaire

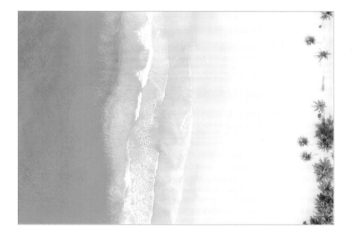

3RD

June

Forever is composed
of nows.

– Emily Dickinson

4TH

June

Love is the only flower that grows and
blossoms without the aid of the seasons.

– Kahlil Gibran

5TH

June

Life must be welcomed with gratitude.

– Luis Sepúlveda

6TH

June

Why do you exist? For no reason: you did not earn it,
you did not even ask for it! It happened.

– Osho

7TH

June

What is it not to sin? Do not ask much;
go, the silent flowers will tell you.

– Angelus Silesius

8TH

June

This is another soothing aspect of nature: its immense beauty is there for everyone. No one can think of taking home a sunrise or a sunset.

– Tiziano Terzani

9TH

June

Every day is a lucky day for an industrious man.

– Buddha

10TH

June

Nature is the source of all true knowledge. She has her own logic,
her own laws; she has no effect without cause nor invention without necessity.

– Leonardo da Vinci

11TH

June

Richness does not lie in the abundance
of goods, but richness is the richness
of the soul.

– *Muhammad*

12TH

June

The ultimate happiness of human
nature consists in peace of body
and soul.

– *Lucius Annaeus Seneca*

13TH

June

On earth there is no heaven, but there are pieces of it.

– Jules Renárd

14TH

June

Without reason no effect is produced in nature;
understand the reason and you will not need experience.

– Leonardo da Vinci

15TH

June

If we go down into ourselves,
we find that we possess exactly
what we desire.

– *Simone Weil*

16TH

June

Our lot in life is to learn.

– *Carlos Castaneda*

17TH

June

The gift of learning to meditate
is the greatest gift you can give yourself
in this lifetime.

– *Sogyal Rinpoche*

18TH

June

An hour sometimes restores us the sum of many years' losses.

– Publilius Syrus

19TH

June

Tenderness and kindness are not signs of weakness and despair,
but manifestations of strength and resolution.

– Kahlil Gibran

20TH

June

I cannot meet the Spring unmoved.
And as she vanishes,
remorse I saw no more of her.

– Emily Dickinson

21ST

June

A summer is always exceptional.

– Gustave Flaubert

22ND

June

Do your little bit of good where you are;
it's those little bits of good put together
that overwhelm the world.

– Desmond Tutu

23RD

June

Clouds come floating into my life,
no longer to carry rain or usher storm,
but to add color to my sunset sky.

– Rabindranath Tagore

24TH

June

Very little is needed
to make a happy life.

– Marcus Aurelius

25TH

June

Life must be lived as play.

– *Plato*

26TH

June

Whatever you can do,
or dream you can, begin it.

– *Johann Wolfgang Goethe*

27TH

June

Don't forget the small things, above all, don't forget the small things.
The smaller the trace, the more important it sometimes is.

– Fyodor Dostoevsky

28TH

June

Do you aspire to great things? Start with little ones.

– Augustine of Hippo

29TH

June

Energy sets us free
and it is the absolute truth.

– *Carlos Castaneda*

30TH

June

The miracle is not to walk on water.
The miracle is to walk on the green
earth, dwelling deeply in the present
moment and feeling truly alive.

– *Thích Nhất Hạnh*

1ST

July

Cultivate the habit of being grateful for every good thing
that comes to you, and to give thanks continuously.
And because all things have contributed to your advancement,
you should include all things in your gratitude.

– Ralph Waldo Emerson

JULY

2ND

July

There is only one thing that
can transform you, that can change you,
and that is awareness.

– Osho

3RD

July

Problems never end,
but neither do solutions.

– Paulo Coelho

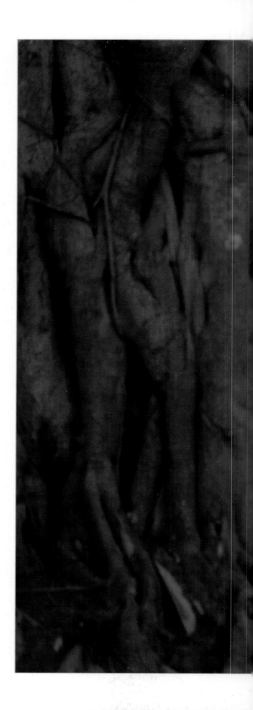

4TH

July

To live is to learn.

– Konrad Lorenz

5TH

July

If a warrior is to succeed at anything, the success must come gently,
with a great deal of effort but with no stress or obsession.

– Carlos Castaneda

6TH

July

That which is not good for the beehive,
cannot be good for the bees.

– Marcus Aurelius

7TH

July

It is such a blessing to live,
and life is so sweet that it cannot be bad.

– Émile Zola

8TH

July

I do not choose where to put an emotion,
I decide to whom I want to give it.

– Alda Merini

9TH

July

After that magic moment when my eyes opened in the sea,
I was no longer able to see, think, or live as before.

– Jacques-Yves Cousteau

10TH

July

A good seed, even if it falls into the sea,
will become an island.

– Malaysian proverb

11TH

July

A heart is a wealth that cannot be sold,
which cannot be bought, but which is given.

– Gustave Flaubert

12TH

July

Children find everything in nothing,
men find nothing in everything.

– Giacomo Leopardi

13TH

July

If you do not have compassion
for yourself, you cannot have
compassion for others.

– *Thích Nhất Hạnh*

14TH

July

A happy life consists
in tranquility of mind.

– *Marcus Tullius Cicero*

15TH

July

He who helps others helps himself.

– Lucius Annaeus Seneca

16TH

July

Only the development of compassion and understanding for others
can bring us the tranquility and happiness we all seek.

– Tenzin Gyatso, 14th Dalai Lama

17TH

July

A happy life must be to a great extent
a quiet life, for it is only in an atmosphere
of quiet that true joy can live.

– Bertrand Russell

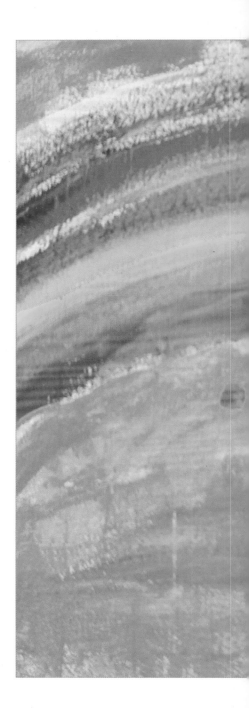

18TH

July

Keep your face always toward
the sunshine, and the shadows
will fall behind you.

— *Anonymous*

19TH

July

The beauty of history, like that of the sea,
lies in what it erases: the incoming wave makes
the trace of the previous one disappear
from the sand.

— *Gustave Flaubert*

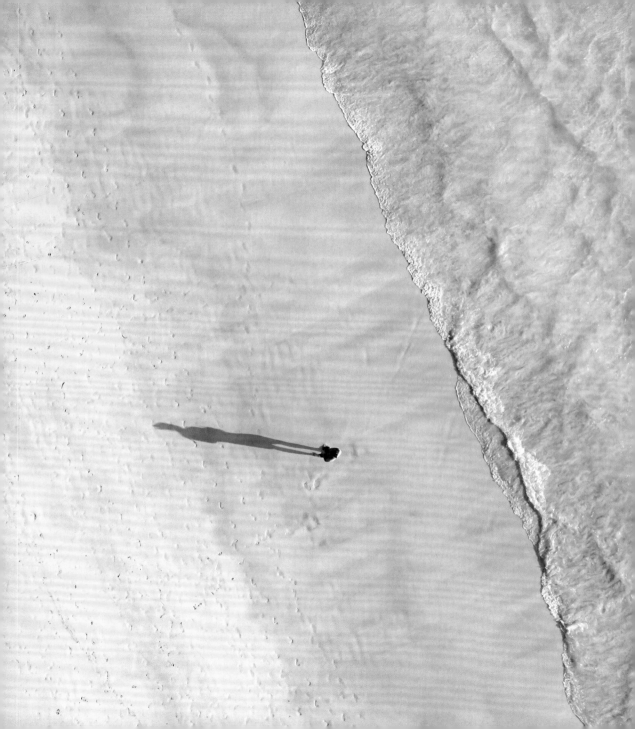

20TH

July

Our own heart is our temple.

– Tenzin Gyatso, 14th Dalai Lama

21ST

July

Some of us think holding on makes us strong;
but sometimes it is letting go.

– *Vincent van Gogh*

22ND

July

Some of us think holding
on makes us strong;
but sometimes it is letting go.

– Hermann Hesse

23RD

July

Have patience with all things,
but chiefly have patience with yourself.

– *Francis de Sales*

24TH

July

Change your thoughts
and you change your world.

– *Norman Vincent Peale*

25TH

July

Freedom is nothing but a chance to be better.

– *Albert Camus*

26TH

July

The course must be decided from the shore,
if you have the ability to do it dexterously;
but when at sea you have to steer with the wind that you have.

– *Alcaeus of Mytilene*

27TH
July

Our real home is The Now.
Living in the present moment
is a miracle.

– Thích Nhất Hạnh

28TH
July

He who wants to do good knocks
at the gate: he who loves finds
the door open.

– Rabindranath Tagore

29TH

July

To love oneself is the beginning
of a lifelong romance.

– *Oscar Wilde*

30TH

July

Love your life, perfect your life,
beautify all things in your life.

– *Tecumseh*

31ST

July

Love yourself. Forgive yourself.
Be true to yourself.
How you treat yourself sets the standard
for how others will treat you.

– *Steve Maraboli*

1ST

August

To me the sea is a continual miracle,
The fishes that swim – the rocks – the motion of the waves –
the ships with men in them,
What stranger miracles are there?

– *Walt Whitman*

AUGUST

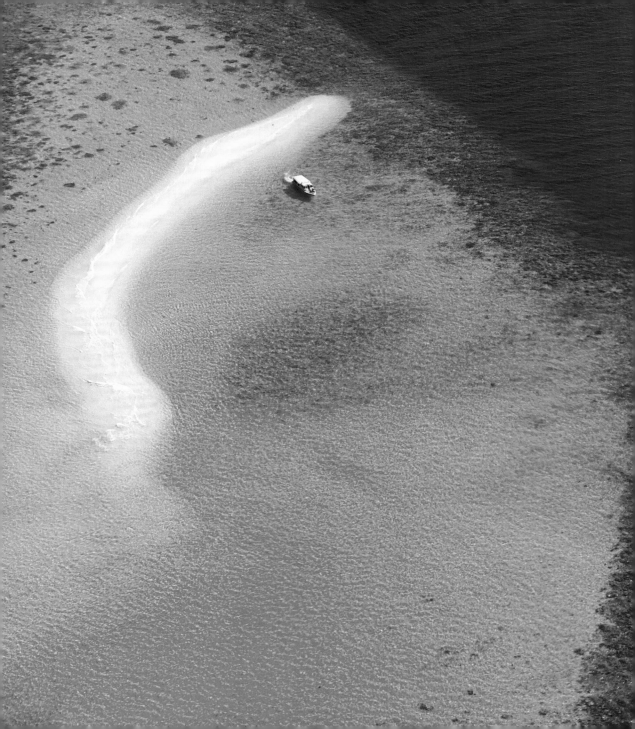

2ND

August

Learn silence. With the calm serenity of a meditative mind,
listen, absorb, transcribe, and transform.

– Pythagoras

3RD

August

I like people who know how to feel the wind on their skin,
smell things, capture the soul.

– Alda Merini

4TH

August

So plant your own gardens
and decorate your soul instead
of waiting for someone
to bring you flowers.

– Jorge Luis Borges

5TH

August

Our bodies are our gardens,
to which our wills are gardeners.

– William Shakespeare

6TH

August

Any day you get up, give thanks for it.

– Sergio Bambarén

7TH

August

Men would be happy
if they hadn't tried and didn't try to be.

– Giacomo Leopardi

8TH

August

What world lies beyond that stormy sea
I do not know, but every ocean
has a distant shore, and I shall reach it.

– Cesare Pavese

9TH
August

The most important decision
you will ever make is to be
in a good mood.

– Voltaire

10TH
August

You can love only
when you are happy.

– Osho

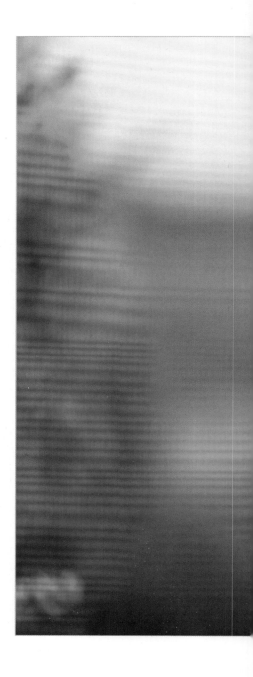

11TH

August

Make your life a rose that speaks silently
in the language of fragrance.

— Sathya Sai Baba

12TH

August

Where strength can only destroy, kindness can sculpt.

– Rabindranath Tagore

13TH
August

Difficult problems are best solved
while they are easy.

— *Lao Tzu*

14TH
August

Although the world is full of suffering,
it is full also of the overcoming of it.

— *Helen Keller*

15TH

August

Chasing after the world brings only chaos.
Allowing it to come to be brings only peace.

– Zen Gatha

16TH

August

Serenity is the final word of all the teachings.

– Hongzhi Zhengjue

17TH

August

Dare to love yourself as if you were
a rainbow with gold at both ends.

– Aberjhani

18TH

August

Patience is necessary, and one cannot
reap immediately where one has sown.

– Søren Kierkegaard

19TH

August

The floating flower ever runs away before
the importunate waves.

– Rabindranath Tagore

20TH

August

There is no month in the whole year in which nature
wears a more beautiful appearance than in the month of August.

– Charles Dickens

21ST

August

Practice kindness all day to everybody
and you will realize you're already in heaven now.

– Jack Kerouac

22ND

August

Every time you smile at someone,
it is an action of love, a gift to that person, a beautiful thing.

– Mother Teresa

23RD

August

Do not think that what is hard for you to master
is humanly impossible; and if it is humanly possible,
consider it to be within your reach.

– *Marcus Aurelius*

24TH

August

Everything is imperfect; there is no sunset so beautiful
that it cannot be more so.

– Fernando Pessoa

25TH

August

Good is the action that causes no regret,
and whose fruit is welcomed
with joy and serenity.

– Buddha

26TH

August

Never be in a hurry; do everything
quietly and in a calm spirit.

– Francis de Sales

27TH

August

Paradise is to love many things
with a passion.

– Pablo Picasso

28TH

August

Every day of life is unique,
but we need something that touches us
to remind us of that.

– Fabio Volo

29TH

August

Sensibility is the most elegant
and precious dress that human
intelligence can wear.

– Osho

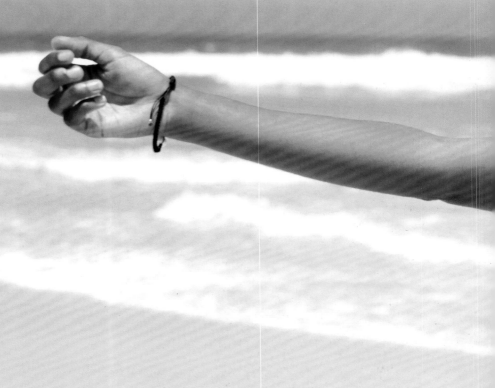

30TH
August

Happiness is an inner rising,
it's an awakening of your energies,
it's an awakening of your soul.

– Osho

31ST
August

Don't forget to love yourself.

– Søren Kierkegaard

1ST

September

"Doing one thing at a time" is how one Zen Master
defined the essence of Zen. Doing one thing at a time means
to be total in what you do, to give it your complete attention.

– Eckhart Tolle

SEPTEMBER

2ND

September

Happiness does not come from owning
a large number of things, but from taking
pride in the work one does.

– Mahatma Gandhi

3RD

September

Just be yourself!

– Osho

4TH

September

Find the sweetness in your own heart,
then you may find the sweetness in every heart.

– Jalal al-Din Rumi

5TH

September

The happiness of your life depends
upon the quality of your thoughts.

– Marcus Aurelius

6TH

September

For nature gives to every time
and season some beauties of its own.

– *Charles Dickens*

7TH

September

The unripe grape, the ripe bunch,
the dried grape, all are changes,
not into nothing, but into something
which exists not yet.

– *Marcus Aurelius*

8TH

September

To create is to live twice.

– *Albert Camus*

9TH

September

There is peace even in the storm.

– Vincent van Gogh

10TH

September

The heart of man is very much like
the sea: it has its storms, it has its tides,
and in its depths it has its pearls too.

– Vincent van Gogh

11TH
September

It made her think that it was curious
how much nicer a person
looked when he smiled.

– *Frances Hodgson Burnett*

12TH
September

This is the very perfection
of a man, to find out
his own imperfections.

– *Augustine of Hippo*

13TH

September

One should be light like a bird,
and not like a feather.

– Paul Valéry

14TH

September

Light is the task where
many share the toil.

– Homer

15TH

September

Free yourself from all thoughts,
be poised in pure Self-awareness.
Don't move from that.

— Ramana Maharshi

16TH

September

A good laugh and a long sleep
are the best cures in the doctor's book.

— Irish proverb

17TH

September

Eternity. It is the sea mingled with the sun.

– *Arthur Rimbaud*

18TH

September

The pale sky slowly changing and flushing and marvelous things happening until the East almost makes one cry out and one's heart stands still at the strange unchanging majesty of the rising of the sun – which has been happening every morning for thousands and thousands and thousands of years.

– Frances Hodgson Burnett

19TH
September

A thing of beauty is a joy forever.

– John Keats

20TH
September

Truth is ever to be found in simplicity
and not in the multiplicity
and confusion of things.

– Isaac Newton

21ST
September

For man, autumn is a time of harvest,
of gathering together.
For nature, it is a time of sowing,
of scattering abroad.

– Edwin Way Teale

22ND
September

Earth provides enough
to satisfy every man's needs,
but not every man's greed.

– Mahatma Gandhi

23RD

September

There is nothing either good or bad,
but thinking makes it so.

– William Shakespeare

24TH

September

Practice good-heartedness
toward all beings.

– Sogyal Rinpoche

25TH

September

A tree with many branches grows
from a tiny sprout.

– *Lao Tzu*

26TH

September

Life is paradise, and we are all
in paradise, but we refuse to see it.

– *Fyodor Dostoevsky*

27TH

September

The mind should not be allowed
to wander toward worldly objects
and what concerns other people.

– Ramana Maharshi

28TH

September

No one is either too young
or too old for the health of the soul.

– Epicurus

29TH
September

In Autumn, don't go to jewelers
to see gold; go to the parks.

— Mehmet Murat Ildan

30TH
September

Everyone must take time
to sit and watch the leaves turn.

— Elizabeth Lawrence

1ST

October

As your mind withdraws from obsessive thinking,
fruitless worrying, and self-recriminations, you feel a sense of refuge.
You have a safe place and it's within.

– Sharon Salzberg

OCTOBER

2ND

October

No one combs my hair
as well as the wind.

– Alda Merini

3RD

October

I cannot endure to waste anything
so precious as autumnal sunshine
by staying in the house.

– Nathaniel Hawthorne

4TH

October

He is richest who is content
with the least, for content
is the wealth of nature.

– Socrates

5TH

October

I could be bounded in a nutshell
and count myself a king of infinite space.

– William Shakespeare

6TH

October

Be clearly aware of the stars and infinity on high.
Then life seems almost enchanted after all.

– Vincent van Gogh

7TH

October

Even the darkest night will end and the sun will rise.

– Victor Hugo

8TH

October

The best practice is meditation,
which, at its essence,
is about stilling the mind.

– *Ramana Maharshi*

9TH

October

Do not go outside,
return to within yourself;
truth dwells in the inner man.

– *Augustine of Hippo*

10TH

October

You earn a lot,
when you lose but learn.

– *Michelangelo Buonarroti*

11TH

October

While we are postponing, life speeds by.

– Lucius Annaeus Seneca

12TH

October

Returning to the source is serenity.

– Lao Tzu

13TH

October

Autumn is a second spring,
when every leaf is a flower.

– Albert Camus

14TH

October

That is the way the leaves fall around
an autumn tree; it is unaware of it,
rain runs down it, it is subjected to sun
or frost and life slowly retreats.
It does not die. It waits.

– Hermann Hesse

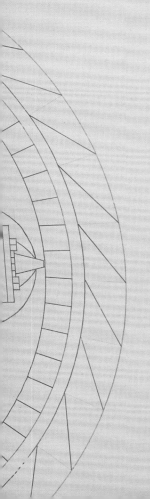

15TH
October

Color in a picture is like
enthusiasm in life.

– Vincent van Gogh

16TH
October

There are no ideal conditions in which to
write, study, work, or reflect, but it is only
the will, passion, and stubbornness that push
a man to pursue his own project.

– Konrad Lorenz

17TH
October

Man's value is in the few things
he creates and not in the many
possessions he amasses.

– Kahlil Gibran

18TH

October

You have to stop to know yourself, to be yourself.

– Tiziano Terzani

19TH

October

How beautiful the leaves grow old.
How full of light and color are their last days.

– John Burroughs

20TH
October

As long as autumn lasts,
I shall not have hands,
canvas, and colors enough to paint
the beautiful things I see.

– Vincent van Gogh

21ST
October

In the autumn one looks at heaven,
in the spring at the earth.

– Søren Kierkegaard

22ND

October

The past has no power over the present moment.

– Eckhart Tolle

23RD

October

There is nothing more visible than what is secret,
and nothing more manifest than what is minute.

– Confucius

24TH

October

Joy is simply being yourself:
alive, vibrant, in full vitality.

– *Osho*

25TH

October

Do not fear life! How beautiful life is,
when you do something good and true!

– *Fyodor Dostoevsky*

26TH

October

Only the light that one kindles
for himself then shines for others as well.

– Arthur Schopenhauer

27TH

October

It is no advantage to be near the light
if the eyes are closed.

– Augustine of Hippo

28TH

October

Don't allow your wounds to transform
you into someone you are not.

– Paulo Coelho

29TH

October

Don't try to make things go
the way you want, but accept them
as they go: you will find peace.

– Epictetus

30TH

October

Don't give up. Normally it is the last key
on the ring which opens the door.

– Paulo Coelho

31ST

October

When one door of happiness closes,
another opens; but often we look so long
at the closed door that we do not see the one
which has been opened for us.

– Helen Keller

1ST

November

The gifts of caring, attention, affection, appreciation,
and love are some of the most precious gifts you can give,
and they don't cost you anything.

– Deepak Chopra

NOVEMBER

2ND

November

November's sky is chill and drear,
November's leaf is red and sear.

– Walter Scott

3RD

November

When the mind is still, the beauty of the Self
is seen reflected in it.

– *B.K.S. Iyengar*

4TH

November

Kindness in words creates confidence.
Kindness in thinking creates profoundness.

– Lao Tzu

5TH

November

For whoever perseveres, the day will come when spiritually
the light will shine around him.

– Rudolf Steiner

6TH

November

Every smile makes you a day younger.

– Chinese proverb

7TH

November

You must never be fearful about
what you are doing when it is right.

– Rosa Parks

8TH

November

Love is unconditional.
Fear is full of conditions.

– Don Miguel Ruiz

9TH

November

Love, and do what you will.

– Augustine of Hippo

10TH

November

A hut where you laugh
is more comfortable than a palace
where you get bored.

– Zen proverb

11TH

November

Looking in itself is not enough,
it is necessary to look with eyes
that want to see, that believe
in what they see.

– Galileo Galilei

12TH

November

I am like a plant that grows
on the bare rock: the more the wind
whips me, the more I plunge my roots.

– Indian proverb

13TH

November

Every danger loses some of its terror
once its causes are understood.

– Konrad Lorenz

14TH

November

You must understand the whole of life,
not just one little part of it. That is why
you must read, that is why you must look
at the skies, that is why you must sing,
and dance, and write poems, and suffer,
and understand, for all that is life.

– Jiddu Krishnamurti

15TH

November

Have patience. All things are difficult
before they become easy.

– Saadi

16TH

November

A tiny change today brings
a dramatically different tomorrow.

– Richard Bach

17TH

November

No matter what the situation,
remind yourself "I have a choice."

– Deepak Chopra

18TH

November

All in all, happiness is a small thing.

– Trilussa

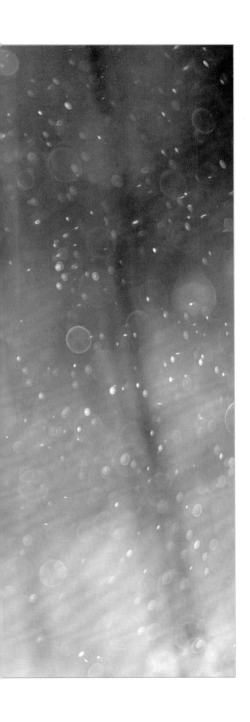

19TH

November

Whenever you are confronted
with an opponent, conquer him with love.

– Mahatma Gandhi

20TH

November

Do not lose your inner peace
for anything whatsoever,
even if your whole world seems upset.

– Francis de Sales

21ST

November

Nothing is more precious than being
in the present moment.
Fully alive, fully aware.

– Thich Nhất Hạnh

22ND

November

It seems to me that
we all look at Nature too much,
and live with her too little.

– Oscar Wilde

23RD

November

Yesterday is gone, tomorrow has not yet come.
We have only today; let us begin.

– Mother Teresa

24TH

November

Even from the same window, no one sees the same things:
the view depends on the gaze.

– Alda Merini

25ᵀᴴ
November

Nothing great is created suddenly,
any more than a bunch of grapes
or a fig. If you tell me that you desire a fig,
I answer you that there must be time.

– Epictetus

26ᵀᴴ
November

One can only forget about time
by making use of it.

– Charles Baudelaire

27TH

November

You take delight not in a city's seven or seventy wonders,
but in the answer it gives to a question of yours.

– Italo Calvino

28TH

November

What's a man's first duty? The answer is brief:
To be himself.

– Henrik Ibsen

29TH
November

There is nothing like returning to a place
that remains unchanged to find the ways
in which you yourself have altered.

– Nelson Mandela

30TH
November

As we work to create light for others,
we naturally light our own way.

– Mary Anne Radmacher

1ST

December

Perhaps there is after all nothing mysterious in Zen.
Everything is open to your full view. If you eat your food
and keep yourself cleanly dressed and work on the farm to raise
your rice or vegetables, you are doing all that is required
of you on this earth, and the infinite is realized in you.

– *Daisetsu Teitarō Suzuki*

DECEMBER

2ND

December

Nature is pleased with simplicity.

– Isaac Newton

3RD

December

Take life lightly, for lightness
is not superficiality, but a gliding
over things from above, without letting
things weigh on your heart.

– Italo Calvino

4TH

December

Not knowing when the dawn will come, I open every door.

– Emily Dickinson

5TH

December

I love snow, snow, and all the forms of radiant frost.

– *Percy Bysshe Shelley*

6TH

December

It is good to be alive because living
is beginning, always, every moment.

– Cesare Pavese

7TH

December

Saying nothing . . .
sometimes says the most.

– Emily Dickinson

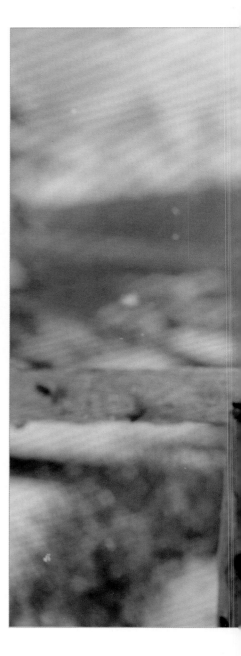

8TH

December

That best portion of a man's life,
his little, nameless, unremembered acts
of kindness and love.

– William Wordsworth

9TH

December

Life's most persistent and urgent question is:
"What are you doing for others?"

– Martin Luther King

10TH

December

It is only in sorrow bad weather masters us;
in joy we face the storm and defy it.

– Amelia Edith Barr

11TH

December

Today let me
and me only
be happy,
with everybody or without them.

– Pablo Neruda

12TH

December

I go to nature to be soothed and healed,
and have my senses put in order.

– John Burroughs

13TH

December

God gave us memory so that we might
have roses in December.

– James Matthew Barrie

14TH

December

Life can only be understood backwards;
but it must be lived forwards.

– Søren Kierkegaard

15TH

December

From the least to the most important event, the affection and respect of others are vital for our happiness.

– Tenzin Gyatso, 14th Dalai Lama

16TH

December

Kindness in giving creates love.

– Lao Tzu

17TH
December

The state we call realization
is simply being oneself.

– Ramana Maharshi

18TH
December

To be yourself is very easy,
you don't have to do a thing.
No effort is necessary.

– Jiddu Krishnamurti

19TH
December

Become such as you are,
having learned what that is.

– Pindar

20TH
December

Choose rather to be strong
of soul than strong of body.

– Pythagoras

21ST

December

There is nothing else so ancient under the sun.
Everything happens for the first time,
but in a way that is eternal.

– *Jorge Luis Borges*

22ND

December

Love comforts like sunshine after rain.

– *William Shakespeare*

23RD

December

Laughter is the sun that drives winter
from the human face.

– Victor Hugo

24TH

December

Take a smile, give it to those
who have never had one.

– Mahatma Gandhi

25TH

December

Give the ones you love wings to fly,
roots to come back, and reasons to stay.

– Tenzin Gyatso, 14th Dalai Lama

26TH

December

In winter, when shade is not needed, the tree loses its leaves.

– Chinese proverb

27TH

December

Nature is painting for us, day after day,
pictures of infinite beauty.

– John Ruskin

28TH

December

Withdraw your mind within,
and you can live anywhere
and under any circumstances.

– Ramana Maharshi

29TH
December

In seed time learn, in harvest teach,
in winter enjoy.

– *William Blake*

30TH
December

For every end, there is always
a new beginning.

– *Antoine de Saint-Exupéry*

31ST

December

Every tick-tock is a second of the life
that passes, flees, and does not repeat
itself. And there is so much intensity,
so much interest, that the problem
is just knowing how to live.

– Frida Kahlo

LIST OF CONTRIBUTORS

A

Aberjhani
(1957 - living)
American writer, historian,
poet, and artist.
(17th August)

Alcaeus of Mytilene
(VII - VI century BCE)
Greek lyric poet.
(26th July)

Allende Isabel
(1942 - living)
Chilean-born American novelist.
(8th April)

Angelus Silesius
(1624 - 1677)
German poet and mystic.
(7th June)

Anonymous
(25th April, 30th April, 18th July)

Arab proverb
(20th March)

Augustine of Hippo
(354 - 430)
Philosopher, theologian, and saint
of the Catholic Church.
(4th April, 28th June, 12th September,
9th October, 27th October, 9th November)

B

Bach Richard
(1936 - living)
American author and aviator.
(16th November)

Bambarén Sergio
(1960 - living)
Peruvian-born Australian author.
(6th August)

Barr Amelia Edith
(1831 - 1919)
British-American writer.
(10th December)

Barrie James Matthew
(1860 - 1937)
British writer.
(13th December)

Battaglia Romano
(1933 - 2012)
Italian author and journalist.
(23rd May)

Baudelaire Charles
(1821 - 1867)
French poet and literary critic.
(25th February, 2nd June,
26th November)

Blake William
(1757 - 1827)
English poet, painter, and printmaker.
(2nd March, 29th December)

Borges Jorge Luis
(1899 - 1986)
Argentine writer, essayist, and poet.
(7th April, 4th August, 21st December)

Bradstreet Anne
(1612 - 1672)
American poet.
(18th January)

Buddha
(566 - 486 BCE)
Indian ascetic and spiritual teacher;
founder of Buddhism.
(4th January, 16th January,
21st February, 9th June, 25th August)

Buonarroti Michelangelo
(1475 - 1564)
Artist and poet, great protagonist
of the Italian Renaissance.
(27th March, 10th October)

Burnett Hodgson Frances
(1849 - 1924)
British writer and playwright.
(16th May, 11th September,
18th September)

Burroughs John
(1837 - 1921)
American poet and naturalist.
(19th October, 12th December)

C

Calvino Italo
(1923 - 1985)
Italian writer and journalist.
(27th November, 3rd December)

Camus Albert
(1913 - 1960)
French author, Nobel Prize
in Literature in 1957.
(25th July, 8th September, 13th October)

Castaneda Carlos
(1925 - 1998)
Peruvian writer.
(2nd February, 16th June, 29th June,
5th July)

Chekhov Anton
(1860 - 1904)
Russian playwright and short-story writer.
(26th February)

Chinese proverb
(12th January, 6th November,
26th December)

Cicero Marcus Tullius
(106 - 43 BCE)
Roman statesman and scholar.
(14th July)

Claudel Paul
(1868 - 1955)
French poet, playwriter, and diplomat.
(10th May)

Coelho Paulo
(1947 - living)
Brazilian writer and poet.
(13th February, 28/29th February,
14th March, 3rd July, 28th October,
30th October)

Confucius
(551 - 479 BCE)
Chinese philosopher.
(15th April, 9th May, 12th May,
23rd October)

Cousteau Jacques-Yves
(1910 - 1997)
French naval officer, oceanographer,
and filmmaker.
(9th July)

D

Darwin Charles
(1809 - 1882)
English naturalist, geologist,
and biologist, best known for his
contributions to evolutionary biology.
(30th May)

De Luca Erri
(1950 - living)
Italian writer, poet, and journalist.
(30th March)

Deepak Chopra
(1946 - living)
Indian physician and writer.
(1st November, 17th November)

Dickens Charles
(1812 - 1870)
English writer and social critic.
(20th August, 6th September)

Dickinson Emily
(1830 - 1886)
American poet.
(3rd June, 20th June, 4th December,
7th December)

Dostoevsky Fyodor
(1821 - 1881)
Russian writer.
(14th April, 20th April, 26th May,
27th June, 26th September,
25th October)

E

Eihei Dōgen
(1200 - 1253)
Japanese Buddhist monk, founder
of Zen Sōtō Buddhist school.
(17th January)

Einstein Albert
(1879 - 1955)
German-born American and Swiss
theoretical physicist; Nobel Prize
in Physics in 1921.
(15th March)

Emerson Ralph Waldo
(1803 - 1882)
American writer and philosopher.
(3rd January, 19th January, 8th February,
5th March, 23rd March, 21st April,
1st July)

Epictetus
(50 - 138)
Greek stoic philosopher.
(2nd May, 29th October,
25th November)

Epicurus
(341 - 270 BCE)
Greek philosopher.
(22nd March, 10th April,
28th September)

F

Flaubert Gustave
(1821 - 1880)
French writer.
(8th January, 7th March, 21st June,
11th July, 19th July)

Mill John Stuart
(1806 - 1873)
British philosopher and economist.
(3rd March, 19th May)

Montale Eugenio
(1896 - 1981)
Italian poet and writer; Nobel Prize
in Literature in 1975.
(29th May)

Mother Teresa
(1910 - 1997)
Albanian-born Indian Catholic nun;
Nobel Peace Prize in 1979.
(10th March, 22nd August,
23rd November)

Muhammad
(571 - 632)
Prophet and founder of Islam.
(11th June)

N
Nepo Mark
(1951 - living)
American poet and philosopher.
(12th April)

Neruda Pablo
(1904 - 1973)
Chilean poet and diplomat; Nobel
Prize in Literature in 1971.
(11th December)

Newton Isaac
(1643 - 1727)
English physicist, mathematician,
astronomer, and philosopher.
(20th September, 2nd December)

Nolan Michael Patrick
(1928 - 2007)
British judge and first chairman of the
Committee on Standards in Public Life.
(6th May)

O
Osho
(1931 - 1990)
Indian mystic, spiritual leader,
and author.
(24th February, 6th June, 2nd July,
10th August, 29th August, 30th August,
3rd September, 24th October)

P
Paine Thomas
(1737 - 1809)
British philosopher and scholar.
(17th March)

Parks Rosa
(1913 - 2005)
American civil rights activist.
(7th November)

Pascoli Giovanni
(1855 - 1912)
Italian poet.
(17th February)

Pavese Cesare
(1908 - 1950)
Italian writer, poet, and translator.
(4th February, 8th August, 6th December)

Peale Norman Vincent
(1898 - 1993)
American writer and preacher.
(24th July)

Pessoa Fernando
(1888 - 1935)
Portuguese poet and writer.
(24th August)

Picasso Pablo
(1881 - 1973)
Spanish sculptor and painter.
(3rd April, 27th August)

Pindar
(6th - 5th century BCE)
Ancient Greek poet.
(19th December)

Pirsig Robert Maynard
(1928 - 2017)
American writer and philosopher.
(20th May)

Plato
(428/427 - 348/347 BCE)
Ancient Greek philosopher.
(25th June)

Pratolini Vasco
(1913 - 1991)
Italian writer.
(22nd February)

Publilius Syrus
(85 - 43 BCE)
Roman playwright.
(18th June)

Pythagoras
(570 - 490 BCE)
Ancient Greek philosopher and
mathematician.
(2nd August, 20th December)

R
Radmacher Mary Anne
(1957 - living)
American writer and artist.
(30th November)

Ramana Maharshi
(1879 - 1950)
Indian mystic, and one of the most
celebrated sages in India of the first
half of the 20th century.
(15th September, 27th September,
8th October, 17th December,
28th December)

Renard Jules
(1864 - 1910)
French writer.
(13th June)

Ricard Matthieu
(1946 - living)
French writer, Buddhist monk.
(2nd January, 13th May)

Ricotti Sonia
(1965 - living)
Canadian entrepreneur, writer, and
training expert in personal and
professional transformation.
(5th May)

Rimbaud Arthur
(1854 - 1891)
French poet.
(17th September)

Rodin Auguste
(1840 - 1917)
French sculptor and painter.
(17th May)

Rogers Carl
(1902 - 1987)
American psychologist.
(14th May)

Roosevelt Eleanor
(1884 - 1962)
American human rights activist and
First Lady of the United States from
1933 to 1945.
(3rd May)

Ruiz Don Miguel
(1952 - living)
Mexican author.
(1st March, 1st May, 8th November)

Rumi Jalal al-Din
(1207 - 1273)
Persian poet, Islamic scholar, mystic.
(7th February, 4th September)

Ruskin John
(1819 - 1900)
English writer, painter, and art critic.
(30th January, 27th December)

Russell Bertrand
(1872 - 1970)
British philosopher, writer, and
mathematician.
(17th July)

S
Saadi
(1210 - 1291 or 1292)
Also known as Saadi Shirazi. Persian
poet and mystic.
(15th November)

Saint-Exupéry Antoine de
(1900 - 1944)
French aviator and writer.
(13th April, 30th December)

Salzberg Sharon
(1952 - living)
American author and teacher
of Buddhist meditation.
(1st October)

Sathya Sai Baba
(1926 - 2011)
Indian spiritual master.
(22nd April, 11th August)

Schopenhauer Arthur
(1788 - 1860)
German philosopher.
(26th October)

Scott Walter
(1771 - 1832)
Scottish writer and novelist.
(2nd November)

Seneca Lucius Annaeus
(4 BCE - 65 CE)
Ancient Roman philosopher.
(3rd February, 13th March, 31st May,
12th June, 15th July, 11th October)

Sepúlveda Luis
(1949 - 2020)
Chilean writer, poet, and political
activist.
(31st March, 5th June)

Shakespeare William
(1564 - 1616)
English poet and playwright.
(18th April, 5th August,
23rd September, 5th October,
22nd December)

Shelley Percy Bysshe
(1792 - 1822)
English romantic poet.
(5th December)

ananda
87 - 1963)
ian physician, yogi, and
losopher.
th January)

crates
0/469 - 399 BCE)
cient Greek philosopher.
October)

gyal Rinpoche
47 - 2019)
etan writer and teacher.
7th June, 24th September)

iner Rudolf
61 - 1925)
strian social reformer and occultist.
h November)

venson Robert Louis
50 - 1894)
ottish writer and poet.
rth April)

n Tzu
4 - 496 BCE)
inese philosopher and strategist.
h April)

zuki Daisetsu Teitarō
870 - 1966)
anese philosopher and historian
religions.
March, 1st December)

gore Rabindranath
61 - 1941)
ngali poet, philosopher, playwright,
d social reformer; Nobel Prize
Literature in 1913.
)th January, 19th April, 23rd June,
th July, 12th August, 19th August)

isen Deshimaru
914 - 1982)
anese Buddhist monk.
5th March)

ale Edwin Way
899 - 1980)
herican naturalist, photographer,
d writer.
lst September)

cumseh
768 - 1813)
awnee Native American chief.
0th July)

Tenzin Gyatso
(1935 - living)
Tibetan Buddhist monk,
14th Dalai Lama.
(16th July, 20th July, 15th December,
25th December)

Terzani Tiziano
(1938 - 2004)
Italian writer and journalist.
(8th June, 18th October)

Thai proverb
(18th March)

Thales of Miletus
(7th - 6th century BCE)
Ancient Greek philosopher.
(14th January, 27th January)

Thich Nhất Hạnh
(1926 - 2022)
Vietnamese Buddhist monk,
peace activist, and author.
(1st April, 30th June, 13th July,
27th July, 21st November)

Thoreau Henry David
(1817 - 1862)
American philosopher, writer,
and poet.
(4th March, 24th May)

Tibetan proverb
(5th February, 12th March)

Tolle Eckhart
(1948 - living)
German spiritual teacher.
(1st January, 11th January, 16th February,
21st March, 1st September, 22nd October)

Trilussa
(1871 - 1950)
Pseudonym of Carlo Alberto Camillo
Salustri, Italian poet and writer.
(18th November)

Tutu Desmond
(1931 - 2021)
South African human rights activist,
Anglican archbishop.
(14th February, 22nd June)

U
Ungaretti Giuseppe
(1888 - 1970)
Italian poet.
(31st January)

V
Valéry Paul
(1871 - 1945)
French writer, poet, and philosopher.
(13th September)

Van Gogh Vincent
(1853 - 1890)
Dutch painter.
(18th February, 21st July, 9th September,
10th September, 6th October,
15th October, 20th October)

Veronesi Umberto
(1925 - 2016)
Italian oncologist and politician.
(15th May)

Vivekananda
(1863 - 1902)
Indian mystic and philosopher.
(29th March, 24th April)

Volo Fabio
(1972 - living)
Pseudonym of Fabio Luigi Bonetti,
Italian actor, writer, and radio and
television personality.
(28th August)

Voltaire
(1694 - 1778)
Nom de plume of François-Marie
Arouet, French philosopher and
writer.
(11th March, 9th August)

W
Watts Alan W.
(1915 - 1973)
British philosopher.
(22nd January)

Weil Simone
(1909 - 1943)
French philosopher and mystic.
(12th February, 9th April, 28th April,
15th June)

Welwood John
(1943 - 2019)
American psychotherapist, teacher,
and author.
(26th April)

Whitman Walt
(1819 - 1892)
American poet, writer, and journalist.
Considered the father of American
poetry.
(22nd May, 1st August)

Wilde Oscar
(1854 - 1900)
Irish poet and writer.
(29th July, 22nd November)

Wordsworth William
(1770 - 1850)
English poet.
(8th December)

Y
Yeats William Butler
(1865 - 1939)
Irish poet, writer, and mystic.
(28th March)

Yourcenar Marguerite
(1903 - 1987)
Pseudonym of Marguerite de
Crayencour, French poet and writer.
(9th February)

Z
Zen Gatha
(15th August)

Zen proverb
(11th February, 10th November)

Zola Émile
(1840 - 1902)
French writer, literary critic, and
journalist.
(7th July)

PHOTO CREDITS

Introduction
Manuela Perugini

Edited
GFB Edit, Sesto San Giovanni (MI)

Project Editor
Valeria Manferto De Fabianis

Graphic Designer
Paola Piacco

Editorial coordination
Giorgio Ferrero

whitestar

WS whitestar™ is a trademark of White Star s.r.l.

© 2024 White Star s.r.l.
Piazzale Luigi Cadorna, 6
20123 Milan, Italy
www.whitestar.it

Editing: Phillip Gaskill

ISBN 978-88-544-2041-0
1 2 3 4 5 6   27 26 25 24 23

Printed in China